Braganza by Robert Jephson

A tragedy. Performed at the Theatre Royal in Drury-Lane

Robert Jephson was born in Ireland in 1736, the son of Archdeacon John Jephson.

His education was at Ryder's grammar school and then the Reverend Roger Ford's school before he was admitted to Trinity College, Dublin in 1751. He left without a degree.

Jephson now joined the British Army with a commission in the 73rd Regiment of Foot. Among his postings was one to the Caribbean. He left, for health reasons and retired with the rank of Captain.

An appointment was offered as master of the horse to the lord-lieutenant of Ireland. Whilst in this office he wrote and had published, in the Mercury newspaper, a collection of articles that defended the lord-lieutenant's administration. These were later published in book form as 'The Bachelor', or 'Speculations of Jeoffry Wagstaffe'.

Jepson held the office under twelve successive viceroys and gained a pension of £300, which was later doubled.

He entered the Irish House of Commons in 1773 and sat for St Johnstown (County Longford) until 1776. Between 1777 and 1783, he served as Member of Parliament for Old Leighlin and thereafter represented Granard from 1783 to 1790

In 1775 he added playwright, dramatist and poet to his military and political career strands. His plays gathered much interest. Among them his tragedy 'Braganza' was successfully performed at Drury Lane in 1775, 'Conspiracy' in 1796, 'The Law of Lombardy' in 1779, and 'The Count of Narbonne' (adapted from Horace Walpole's 'The Castle of Otranto') at Covent Garden in 1781.

In 1788 he published 'Extempore Ludicrous Miltonic Verses' and, in 1794, the heroic poem 'Roman Portraits', and 'The Confessions of Jacques Baptiste Couteau', a satire on the excesses of the French Revolution.

Robert Jephson died at Blackrock, near Dublin, on the 31st of May 1803.

Index of Contents

DEDICATION

TO LADY VISCOUNTESS NUNEHAM.

MADAM,

I HAVE many reasons to be flattered with the public reception of this Tragedy, yet I confess my solicitude for its reputation extends further.

Your Ladyship's having permitted me the honour of inscribing it to you, will in some measure gratify my ambition by recommending it to the reader, whose judgment is not influenced by the adventitious assistance of theatrical decorations and the graces of action.

Where your Ladyship's name appears as a patroness, merit will be expected; and where there is a wish to find any, probably none will pass unnoticed.

Whatever motive may be assigned for this Address, my principal purpose will be fully answered if your Ladyship accepts it, as a testimony of my gratitude for the favours I have received from the Noble Family to which you are so happily united, and of the perfect esteem and respect of

MADAM,

Your Ladyship's Much obliged and Most obedient Humble Servant, ROBERT JEPHSON.

Dublin Castle, Febr. 1775.

DRAMATIS PERSONAE

Don Juan, Duke of Braganza	Mr. Reddish.
Almada	Mr. Aickin.
Ribiro	Mr. Palmer.
Mendoza	Mr. Brereton.
Antonio	Mr. Wrighten.

Mello	Mr. Wheeler.
Roderic	Mr. Wright.
Ferdinand	Mr. Norris.
Lemos	Mr. Usher.
Corea	Mr. Hurst.
Velasquez, Minister of Spain	Mr. Smith.
Pizarro	Mr. Davies.
Ramirez	Mr. Packer.
Officer	Mr. Keen.
First Citizen	Mr. Wright.
Second Citizen	Mr. Griffiths.
Ines	Mrs. Johnston.
Louisa, Dutchess of Braganza	Mrs. Yates.

Gentlemen, Attendants, Soldiers, &c.

SCENE: LISBON

BRAGANZA; A TRAGEDY

PROLOGUE

Written by ARTHUR MURPHY, Esq.
SPOKEN BY MR. PALMER.

While in these days of sentiment and grace
Poor comedy in tears resigns her place,
And smit with novels, full of maxims crude,
She, that was frolick once, now turns a prude;
To her great end the tragic muse aspires,
At Athens born, and faithful to her sires.
The comic sister in hysteric fit,
You'd swear, has lost all memory of wit.
Folly, for her, may now exult on high;
Feather'd by ridicule no arrows fly;
But if you are distress'd, she's sure to cry.
She that could jig, and nick-name all heav'n's creatures,
With sorrows not her own deforms her features;
With stale reflections keeps a constant pother;
Greece gave her one face, and she makes another;
So very pious, and so full of woe,
You well may bid her "To a nunnery go."
Not so Melpomene; to nature true
She holds her own great principle in view.
She, from the first, when men her pow'r confest,

When grief and terror seiz'd the tortur'd breast,
She made, to strike her moral to the mind,
The stage the great tribunal of mankind.
Hither the worthies of each clime she draws,
Who founded states, or rescued dying laws;
Who, in base times, a life of glory led,
And for their country who have toil'd or bled;
Hither they come, again they breathe, they live,
And virtue's meed through ev'ry age receive.
Hither the murd'rer comes, with ghastly mien!
And the fiend conscience hunts him o'er the scene.
None are exempted; all must re-appear,
And even kings attend for judgement here;
Here find the day, when they their pow'r abuse,
Is a scene furnish'd to the tragic muse.
Such is her art, weaken'd perhaps at length,
And, while she aims at beauty, losing strength.
Oh! when resuming all her native rage,
Shall her true energy alarm the stage?
This night a bard—(our hopes may rise too high,
'Tis yours to judge;—'tis yours the cause to try)
This night a bard, as yet unknown to fame,
Once more, we hope, will rouze the genuine flame.
His; no French play;— tame, polish'd, dull by rule!
Vigorous he comes, and warm from Shakespeare's school.
Inspir'd by him, he shews, in glaring light,
A nation struggling with tyrannic might;
Oppression rushing on with giant strides;
A deep conspiracy, which virtue guides;
Heroes, for freedom who dare strike the blow,
A tablature of honour, guilt and woe.
If on his canvass nature's colours shine,
You'll praise the hand that trac'd the just design.

ACT I

SCENE I. A Piazza

RIBIRO meeting a Spanish **OFFICER** conducting **TWO CITIZENS** bound. **LEMOS** and **COREA** following RIBIRO at a little Distance.

RIBIRO
Hold, officer—What means this spectacle?
Why lead you thus in fetters thro' the streets
These aged citizens?

OFFICER
Behold this order. shews a paper.

RIBIRO
I know the character. 'Tis signed Velasquez.

1st CITIZEN
We have not mines of unexhausted gold
To feed rapacious Spain and stern Velasquez;
And wrung by hard exactions for the state—

OFFICER
No more—I must not suffer it—

RIBIRO [Pointing to the prisoners]
Pray, Sir—
See these white hairs, these shackles—Misery
May sure complain—You are a soldier, Sir,
Your mien bespeaks a brave one—

OFFICER
I will walk by.
Detain them not too long—'Tis a harsh sentence.

[**OFFICER** withdraws a little.

2nd CITIZEN.
O good Ribiro, what have we deserved,
That these rude chains shou'd gall us?

RIBIRO
What deserved!

1st CITIZEN
The little all our industry had earn'd,
To smooth the bed of sickness, nurse old age,
And give a decent grave to our cold ashes,
Spain's hungry minions have already seized.—

RIBIRO
I know the rest—Dry up these scalding tears—
The hour of your deliv'rance is at hand:
—An arm more strong than shuts your prison doors,
Shall burst them soon, and give you ample vengeance.

CITIZENS
May we indeed expect—

RIBIRO
—Most sure—But hush—
Resume the semblance of this transient shame,
And hide your hope in sadness—Brave Castilian,
Thanks for this courtesy. To the Officer, who returns.

CITIZENS
Lead on—Farewell.

[Exeunt **GUARD** and **CITIZENS**.

[**LEMOS** and **COREA** come forward to **RIBIRO.**

RIBIRO
Was that a fight for Lisbon?

LEMOS
O shame! shame!
What crime cou'd they commit?—Old, helpless, plunder'd—

RIBIRO
—Even thoughts are crimes in this distemper'd state.
They once had wealth as you have—Spain thought meet
To seize it—They (rash men) have dar'd to murmur.
Velasquez here—our scourge—King Philip's idol,
Whom Portugal must bow to—mildly dooms them,
But to perpetual bondage for this treason.

LEMOS
We must be patient—'Tis a cureless evil.

RIBIRO
Is patience then the only virtue left us?
Come, come, there is a remedy more manly.

COREA
Wou'd it were in our reach!

RIBIRO
Look here, I grasp it.
Laying his hand on his sword.
What turned to statues! — Hence enfranchisement
If the quick fire that lately warm'd your breasts,
Already wastes to embers.—Am I rash?
We touch'd this theme before—You felt it then.
Wou'd I cou'd put a tongue in every ingot,
That now lies pil'd within your massy stores—
Your gold perhaps might move you—Spain will seize it,

Then bid you mourn the loss in the next dungeon,
Or dig her mines for more—Is't not enough?—
Instruct me, Lemos, you, good Corea, teach me
This meekness so convenient to our foes,
Or pierce this swelling bosom.

LEMOS
Who can teach it?
'Tis not in art Ribiro—Know us better.
The canker discontent consumes within,
And mocks our smooth exterior.

COREA
Hear me for both:
For all th' indignant hearts in Portugal—
If curses sped like plagues and pestilence,
Thus wou'd I strike them at the towers of Spain.
May her swoln pride burst like an empty bubble?
Distraction rend her councils, route and shame
Pursue her flying squadrons—Tempests scatter
And whirlpools swallow up her full man'd navies!
Bold insurrection spread thro' all her states,
Shaking like pent-up winds their loose allegiance!
All Europe arm, and every frowning king,
Point at one foe, and let that foe be Spain!

RIBIRO
O be that curse prophetic!—Here 'tis dangerous,
Nor will the time allow to tell you all.
But thus far rest assured; — I speak not rashly —
A project is on foot, and now just rip'ning,
Will give our indignation nobler scope,
Than tears or curses (priests and womens weapons.)
All that secures the event of great designs,
Sage heads, firm hearts, and executing arms,
In formidable union league with us,
And chain capricious fortune to our standard.

LEMOS
Say, can our aid promote this glorious cause?

RIBIRO
All private virtue is the public fund:
As that abounds, the state decays, or thrives;
Each shou'd contribute to the general stock,
And who lends most, is most his country's friend.

LEMOS

O wou'd Braganza meet the people's wish!

RIBIRO
He is not yet resolved,—but may be won—
Cou'd I assure him men like you but wish'd it,
(For well he knows and loves you) — Trust me, Lemos!
It wou'd do more to knit him to this cause,
Than legions of our hot nobility.

COREA
We love his virtue—will support his rights—

RIBIRO
Then shew it by your deeds.—Your artizans
Are prompt, bold, hardy, fond of violence.
Alarm their slumb'ring courage, rouse their rage,
Wake their dulled senses to the shame and scorn
That hisses in the ears of willing bondmen;
If they will hazard one bold stroke for freedom,
A leader shall be found, a brave—a just one.
Anon expect me where the ivied arch
Rears the bold image of our late Braganza.
In sullen discontent he seems to frown
As if still hostile to the foes of Lisbon.
There we'll discourse at large—Almada comes—

LEMOS
Is he a friend?

RIBIRO
A firm one—No dishonour
E'er bow'd that rev'rend head—That mighty spirit
When first the oppressor, like a flood, o'erwhelm'd us,
Rear'd high his country's standard and defied him.
—He comes to seek me—Lose no time—Remember.

[Exeunt **LEMOS** and **COREA**.

RIBIRO [Alone]
I shou'd detest my zeal, cou'd it be stir'd
Against the wholesome rigour of restraint
Licentiousness made needful—But good Heaven!
Foul murders unprovok'd, delib'rate cruelty—
—The God within us must rise up against it.

[Enter **ALMADA**.

ALMADA

Well met Ribiro—What new proselytes?
Thy ardor every hour, or finds, or makes them.

RIBIRO
No—thank the Spaniards for our proselytes—
Scarce half an hour ago, two citizens
(My blood still boils) by fell Velasquez order
Were drag'd to prison—

ALMADA
Spare my soul, Ribiro,
Superfluous detestation of that villain.

RIBIRO
Knowing this way they were to pass, I brought
Lemos and Corea (whom last night I founded)
That their own eyes might see the outrages,
Men of their order must expect to meet
From power that knows no bounds, and owns no law.

ALMADA
'Twas wisely done; for minds of coarse alloy
But bluntly feel the touch of others wrongs,
Tho' deep they take the impression of their own.

RIBIRO
By heav'n their fury bore a nobler stamp;
Their honest rage glow'd on their kindling cheeks,
Broke thro' the cold restraints of coward caution,
And swell'd even to an eloquence of anger.

ALMADA
'Tis well—But are they yet inform'd how near
Th' approaching hour, decisive of our fate,
That gives us death or freedom—that the dawn—

RIBIRO
Not yet —They still believe the Duke at noon
But visits Lisbon to command the march
Of our new levies, to the Spanish bounds;
Himself to follow streight—Ere then I mean
Again to see them, and still more to whet
The keeness of their hate against our tyrants.
—At least a thousand follow where they lead—

ALMADA
Their boldness well directed may do much.

RIBIRO

That care be mine—I've studied—and I know them;
Inconstant, sanguine, easily inflam'd,
But like the nitrous powder uncompress'd,
Consuming by the blaze nought but itself.
'Tis ours to charge the mine with deadly skill,
And bury usurpation in the ruin.

ALMADA

I think we cannot fail—Our friends are firm.
Honour will bind the noble—Hope the weak,
And common interest all—The insulting Spaniard
Broods over embryo mischiefs, nor suspects
The wretched worm conceals a mortal sting
To pierce the haughty heel that tramples him.

RIBIRO

How great will be our triumph, Spain's disgrace,
When ev'ry mischief that perfidious court
Has fram'd against Braganza's precious life,
Recoils on the contriver!

ALMADA

Urge that home;
Urge how the Duke's affection to his country,
His right unquestionable to her crown,
First mark'd him for the victim of false Spain;
That his commission as high admiral,
His general's staff, and all the lofty pomp
Of his high sounding titles, were but meant
As gilded snares to invite him to his death.

RIBIRO

These truths, shameful to Philip, must be told;
They will endear Don Juan to the people,
Will keep them waking, restless, and dispos'd
To aid the glorious tumult of to-morrow.

ALMADA

My heart expands, and with a prophet's fire
Seizes the bright reversion of our hopes.
I see the genius of our realm restor'd,
And smiling lead him to his rightful throne.
No wild ambition, like a pamper'd steed,
O'erleaps the boundaries of law and reason,
And tramples every seed of social virtue:
But o'er the temp'rate current of his blood
The gentlest passions brush their breezy wings,

To animate, but not disturb the stream.
Such is his temper—The approaching hour
Demands perhaps a sterner.

RIBIRO
Heaven still kind,
Has in his confort's breast struck deep the root
Of each aspiring virtue.—Bright Louisa,
To all the softness of her tender sex,
Unites the noblest qualities of man;
A genius to embrace the amplest scheme
That ever swell'd the labouring statesman's breast;
Judgment most sound, persuasive eloquence
To charm the froward and convince the wise;
Pure piety without religion's dross,
And fortitude that shrinks at no disaster.

ALMADA
She is indeed a wonder.— O Ribiro,
That woman was the spring that mov'd us all.
She canvass'd all our strength, urged all our wrongs,
Combin'd our force, and methodized our vengeance.
Taught us that ends which seem impossible
Are lost, or compass'd only by the means;
That fortune is a false divinity,
But folly worships what the wise man makes.
She turn'd our cold dejection to device,
And rous'd despondency to active valour.
My age delights to dwell on her perfections —

RIBIRO
And I could ever hear them—Virtue's praise
To honest ears is music. — But no more—
A noise comes this way, and that hurrying throng
Proclaims the upstart Minister's approach.
This is the hour with fancy pageantry
Thro' our thin'd streets he takes his wonted round;
Like the dire clapping of the harpy's wing,
To choak the frugal meal with bitter tears,
And scare content from every humble board.
I will avoid him. But I go, proud man,
When next we meet to make my presence dreadful.

[Exit **RIBIRO**.

ALMADA [Alone]
Honest Ribiro!—To this hour my soul
Has kept her purpose; my firm foot has ne'er

Swerv'd from its path in Lisbon, nor shall now
Give way to insolence.—Your country's dregs!
Looking towards the train of Velasquez.
Ye supple sycophants! Ay, cringe and beg
That he will tread upon your prostrate necks,
Or ride you like his mules.—Authority!
Thy worship'd symbols round a villain's trunk
Provoke men's mockery, not their reverence.

[**OFFICER** entering.

Make way there—room, room for the Minister.
Know you the lord Velasquez comes this way?
[To **ALMADA**]
Pray, Sir, give place.

ALMADA
Officious varlet, off!
Let not thy servile touch pollute my robe.
Can hirelings frown?—

[Enter **VELASQUEZ** and **PIZARRO**—The Magistrates of Lisbon with their Insignia, **GUARDS** and
ATTENDANTS preceding.

VELASQUEZ [Looking sternly at **ALMADA**]
How! Am I then despised—
A tumult in my presence:—Good, my lord,
It better wou'd become your gravity,
To set the fair example of obedience
To trust and office, than instruct the rabble
In what they are the most prone to, feuds and faction.

ALMADA
Most reverend admonition! Hold my spleen!
Ye golden coronets and ermin'd robes,
Bend from your stools, behold this wond'rous man,
This Lusitanian censor, this sage Cato,
This consul, with his lictors, rods and axes,
Reprove the boy, Almada, for his lightness!

PIZARRO
Regard not his wild words, he's old and choleric.

VELASQUEZ [To his train]
Attend me at the citadel—Move on. Exeunt attendants.
I know not whether to accuse my fortune,
Or blame my own demerits; brave Almada,
That ever when we meet, thy angry brow

Rebukes me with its frown, or keen reproach
Darts from thy tongue, and checks the forward wish
That fain wou'd court thy friendship and esteem.

ALMADA
Friendship with thee!—Is it so slight a boon?
If such deserve the name, go seek for friends
Amidst the desp'rate crew whose only bond
Is the black conscience of confederate crimes;
Nor in prepost'rous union think to join
Integrity with guilt, and shame with honour.
Know me for what I am—thy foe profess'd.
Fall on thy knee—solicit Heaven for mercy,
And tell that seat of pride, thy obdurate he art,
Its last, its only virtue is—remorse.—

[Exit **ALMADA**.

[Manent **VELASQUEZ** and **PIZARRO**.

VELASQUEZ
Go, hoary fool! preach to the whistling winds,
I scorn thy council, and defy thy hate.
'Tis time enough for lagging penitence,
When age, like thine, has quench'd ambition's flame.
Now nobler thoughts possess my active soul.
This haughty province first shall feel my weight,
And since it scorns my love, thro' fear obey me.

PIZARRO
Already all the power of Spain is thine,
The Vice Queen, Marg'ret, tho' of Austrian blood,
Discreet, firm, virtuous, complains in vain;
You leave her but a regent's empty title,
While power is only yours:—And happier still,
Braganza summon'd to attend the King,
Will soon cut off his country's only hope,
And leave no rival to obscure thy lustre.
'Bate but the shew and name of royalty,
Thou art already King.

VELASQUEZ
The shew, the name,
All that gives grace and awe to majesty
Shall soon be mine, Pizarro—Olivarez,
Whose counsels rule the Escurial, to my hand
Has long resign'd the reins of Portugal,
And dreams not (unsuspicious of my faith)

The Delegate, the creature of his breath,
Anon will bid defiance to his power,
And rank himself with monarchs.

PIZARRO
O take heed,
Consider, Sir, that power still awes the world—

VELASQUEZ
My towering fortune rises on a rock,
And firm as Atlas will defy the storm.
The purple cement of a Prince's blood
Shall strengthen its foundation.

PIZARRO
Ha!

VELASQUEZ
Braganza's.
—The precious mischief swells my exulting breast,
And soon shall burst its prison.

PIZARRO
Can it be?
I know thy dauntless temper mocks at fear,
And prudence guides thy daring.—But a Prince
Follow'd by faithful guards—encompass'd round
With troops of gallant friends—the people's idol—

VELASQUEZ
Is mortal, like the meanest of his train,
And dies before to-morrow.—Cease to wonder—
But when this mighty ruin shakes the realm,
Prepare like me, with well-dissembled grief,
To hide our real joy, and blind suspicion.
Flourish of trumpets.
These trumpets speak his entrance; never more
Such sprightly notes, nor shout of joyful friends,
Paean or choral song shall usher him;
But sad solemnity of funeral pomp,
Mute sorrow, mournful dirges, ghastly rites,
Marshal'd by death, in comfortless array,
Wait his cold relics to their sepulchre.

An Anti-chamber in the Duke of Braganza's Palace

RIBIRO, **MENDOZA**.

RIBIRO
A Moment's pause, Mendoza! here appointed
By promise to the Duke at noon to wait him,
I could not mingle with his followers,
So saw it but in part—

MENDOZA
The air still rings
With loudest acclamations.

RIBIRO
Yes, Mendoza;
With joy I heard them—heard the vaulted sky
Echo Braganza.—'Twas no hireling noise,
No faction's roar of mercenary joy,
Sound without transport—but the heart-felt cry
Of a whole nation's welcome. Hear it Spain!
Proud usurpation hear it!

MENDOZA
The whole way
Was cover'd thick with panting multitudes,
That scarce left passage for their chariot wheels;
The trees were bent with people; ev'ry roof,
Dome, temple, portico, so closely fill'd,
The gazers made the wonder. Here and there
A discontented Spaniard stalk'd along
Should'ring the crowd; and with indignant scorn
Turn'd up his sallow cheek in mockery.

RIBIRO
We shall retort their scorn—Mark'd you the Duke?
His mind is ever letter'd in his face.

MENDOZA
Pleasure was mingled with anxiety,
Both visible at once. But, O what words
Can paint the angel form that grac'd his side,
His bright Louisa! like th' Olympian Queen,
When o'er her fragrant bosom Venus bound
Th' enchanting Cestus—from her lucid eyes
Stream'd the pure beams of soft benevolence,

And glories more than mortal shone around her.
Harmonious sounds of dulcet instruments
Swell'd by the breath, or swept from tuneful wire,
Floated in air—while yellow Tagus burn'd
With prows of flaming gold; their painted flags
In gandy frolick fluttering to the breeze.
On to their palace thus the triumph came:
Alighted at the gate, the princely pair
Express'd their thanks in silent dignity
Of gesture, far more eloquent than words;
Then turn'd them from the throng—

RIBIRO
Why this looks well.
The Duke will sure be rous'd to resolution
By this bright presage of his coming glory.

MENDOZA
With grief I learn he still is undetermin'd.
His fears prevail against the public wish;
And thus the ill-pois'd scale of our fair hopes,
Mounts light and unsubstantial.

RIBIRO
O you wrong him.
I know his noble nature—Juan's heart
Pants not with selfish fear—His wife, his friends,
An infant family, a kingdom's fate,
More than his own, besiege his struggling soul;
He must be more than man, who will not hear
Such powerful calls, and less, who can despise them.

MENDOZA
Indeed I cannot wonder he's disturb'd,
But doubts are treason in a cause like this.

RIBIRO
Dismiss these fears—Louisa's gentle sway
Will fix him to our purpose. Night's chaste orb
Rules not the heavings of the restless tide,
More sure than she with mild ascendancy
Can govern all his ebbs and flows of passion.
But come, by this time the fond multitude
Have gaz'd away their longing, and retire.
Our greeting will be seasonable now.

[Exeunt.

A magnificent Chamber in the Duke of Braganza's Palace

The **DUKE** speaking to **LEMOS** and **COREA**—Other **CITIZENS** at a little Distance.

DUKE
No more kind countrymen—This goodness melts me.
What can I render back for all these honours?
This wond'rous prodigality of praise?
What but my life, whene'er your wellfare asks it.

LEMOS
Heav'n guard that precious life for Portugal!
To you, as to a tutelary God,
This sinking country lifts her suppliant hands,
And certain of your strength, implores your arm
To raise her prostrate genius from the dust.

DUKE
A private man, a subject like yourselves,
Bankrupt of power, though rich in gratitude—
The sense of what you suffer wrings my soul,
Nor makes your sorrows less.

DUTCHESS
Much injur'd men
Whom love not fear should govern—from this hour
Know we espouse your cause—We have not hearts
Of aliens, to behold with passing glance
And cold indifference, the ruthless spoiler
Smile o'er the ravage of your fertile plains.
We feel the fetters that disgrace your limbs;
We mourn the vigour of your minds depress'd:
With horror we behold your gen'rous blood,
Drain'd by the infatiate thirst of ravening wolves.
If we have nature, we must feel your wrongs,
If we have power, redress them—

COREA
Matchless lady!
There spoke our rightful Queen, our better angel!
In us behold your servants, subjects, soldiers;
Though yet unpractis'd in the trade of war,
Our swords will find an edge at your command.

DUKE
We neither doubt your courage nor your love,
And both perhaps ere long may meet the trial—
I would detain you—but our conference,
Might now be dangerous—Rank me with your friends,
And know I have a heart for Portugal.

[Exeunt **LEMOS**, **COREA**, &c.

[Manent **DUKE** and **DUTCHESS**.

DUTCHESS
Why wears my Juan's brow that thoughtful cloud
Why thus with downcast look and folded arms?
When ev'ry other bosom swells with hope,
When expectation, like a fiery steed,
Anticipates the course, and pants to hear
The sprightly signal start him for the goal.
Think that the people from their leader's eye
Catch the sure omens of their future fate;
With his their courage falls, their spirits rise;
For confidence is conquest's harbinger.

DUKE
Light of thy Juan's life! My soul's best joy?
Swifter than meteors glide, or wings of wind,
My nimble thoughts shoot thro' their whirling round:
A thousand cares distract this anxious breast.
To recompense the dark uncertainty
Of this dread interval, 'twixt now and morn,
Would ask whole years of happiness to come.
Now thou art mine, these faithful arms enfold thee;
But oh! to-morrow may behold thee torn
By barbarous ruffians from their fond embrace,
The flowing honours of that beauteous head,
May sweep a scaffold's dust, and iron death
Close in eternal sleep those radiant eyes
That beam with love and joy unutterable.

DUTCHESS
O make me not your curse, as sure I must be,
The stain, the blot of your immortal fame,
If one soft passion like a languid spell,
Dissolve thy manly fortitude of soul,
And melt the prince and patriot in the husband.

DUKE
That tender union is the healing balm,

The cordial of my soul—our destinies
Are twin'd together—Were my single life
The only forfeit of this perilous chance,
I'd throw it, like a heedless prodigal,
And wanton with my fortune—But alas!
More than the wealth of worlds is now at stake.
And can I hazard this dear precious pledge,
Venture my all of bliss on one bold cast,
Nor feel the conflict that now rends my heart?

DUTCHESS
Why do you tremble?—These cold struggling drops—

DUKE
—They fall for thee Louisa—my quell'd spirit
Avows its weakness there—

DUTCHESS
'Tis cruel fondness,
It wounds me deeply Juan.

DUKE
Witness honour!
Thy martial call ne'er found Braganza's ear
Cold, till this bitter moment.—I have met,
Nay courted death, in the steel'd files of war,
When squadrons wither'd as the giant trod;
Nor shrunk ev'n when the hardiest in the field
Have paused upon the danger—Here, I own,
My agonizing nerves degrade the soldier,
Ev'n to a coward's frailty—Should the sword
Which black destruction soon may wave o'er all,
(Avert it Heaven!) strike at thy precious life,
Should but one drop, forc'd by rude violence,
Stain that dear bosom, I were so accurs'd,
The outstretch'd arm of mercy could not save me.

DUTCHESS
I have a woman's form, a woman's fears,
I shrink from pain and start at dissolution.
To shun them is great Nature's prime command;
Yet summon'd as we are, your honour pledg'd,
Your own just rights engag'd, your country's fate,
Let threat'ning death assume his direst form,
Let dangers multiply, still would I on,
Still urge, exhort, confirm thy constancy,
And though we perish'd in the bold attempt,
With my last breath I'd bless the glorious cause,

And think it happiness to die so nobly.

DUKE
O thou hast roused me—From this hour I banish
Each fond solicitude that hover'd round thee:
Thy voice,—thy looks—thy soul are heav'n's own fire.
'Twere impious but to doubt that pow'r ordain'd thee
To guide me to this glorious enterprize:

DUTCHESS
Thou shalt be chronicl'd to latest time,
Heaven's chosen instrument to punish tyrants.
The great restorer of a nation's freedom!
Thou shalt complete what Brutus but attempted.
Nor withering age, nor cold oblivion's shade,
Nor envy's cank'rous tooth shall blast thy wreaths:
But every friend to virtue shall inscribe
To Juan's name eternal monuments.
But see our friends approach — a-while I leave thee—
Remember still—thou must be king or nothing.

[Exit **DUTCHESS**.

DUKE [Alone]
I will suppress th' emotions of my heart.
Quite to subdue them is impossible.

[Enter **RIBIRO** and **MENDOZA.**

Welcome ye wakeful guardians of your country!
Had we in all the people's mighty mass
But twenty spirits match'd with you in virtue,
How might we bid defiance to proud Spain;
How scorn the close disguise of secret councils,
And challenge their full force in open combat!

RIBIRO
Led by Don Juan, can we doubt th' event?
All things conspire—Antipathy to Spain
Is here hereditary—'Tis nature's instinct,
'Tis principle, religion, vital heat.
Old men to list'ning sons with their last breath
Bequeath it as a dying legacy.
Infants imbibe it at the mother's breast.
It circles with their blood, spreads with their frame,
Its fountain is the heart, and till that fails
The stream it fed can never cease to flow.

MENDOZA
That furious impulse gives the spleen of fiends
To softest tempers, the unpractis'd arm
Sinews with lion's strength, and drives us on
Resistless as the sweeping whirlwind's force.

DUKE
All is propitious! Every post is fill'd
With officers devoted to our service:
Already in their hearts they own my title,
And wait but for our orders to proclaim it.

[Enter **ALMADA.**

DUKE
Come to my breast, my sage admonisher!
The tutor and example of my arms!
The proud Iberian soon shall feel their force;
And learn from Juan's sword to venerate
The fame of brave Almada.

ALMADA
Thus my prince,
Thus did I hope to find thee. Hence no more
Shall hard exactions grind the prostrate people;
Our gentry to their provinces confin'd
Languish no more in shameful circumscription;
No more our ancient noblemen be stripp'd
Of all but empty titles, tinsel names
Like tarnish'd gold on rags to mock the wearer!
Our posts of eminence no more be filled
With upstart strangers, or the sordid lees
Of base plebian natives—

DUKE
My impatient breast,
Full of the expected joy, like a young bridegroom,
Upbraids the lazy hours that lag between
My wishes and enjoyment—The onset is—

ALMADA
When St. Lazar beats five, about that hour
We'll welcome the sun's rising with an offering
More glorious than the Persians Hecatomb.

RIBIRO
At night your friends assemble with Almada
In dreadful secrecy — Then with rais'd arm

We rush to cancel our long debt to vengeance,
And glut our thirsty blades with Spanish gore.

ALMADA
If we suspend the blow beyond to-morrow
All may be lost — Three thousand veterans
Lye canton'd on the river's southern side;
Should our design be known, they will be call'd
To reinforce the posts, and guard the city.
Adieu then to our dream of liberty!
We rivet closer chains on Portugal,
And drag the doom of traytors on ourselves.

[Enter **DUTCHESS.**

DUTCHESS
Suspend your consultations for a moment,
Within the minister of Spain attends;
Forgive th' officious love of your Louisa:
No stranger to his arts, she warns her Juan—

DUKE
I know he comes in solemn mockery
To make a hollow tender of his service
With most obsequious falshood.

DUTCHESS
My best Lord,
Hold strictest watch on all your words and motions;
Guard every look, with that discerning villain;
Subtle, infiduous, false, and plausible;
He can with ease assume all outward forms,
Seem the most honest, plain, sincere good man,
And keep his own designs lock'd close within,
While with the lynx's beam he penetrates
The deep reserve of every other breast.

DUKE
I too will wear my vizor in the scene,
And play the dupe I am not.—Friends, farewell!
Perhaps ere morning we may meet again—
The hour is fix'd, Louisa;—all prepar'd—

DUTCHESS
Then this is our last night of slavery—
A brighter aera rises with the dawn. Exit Duke.
If we may dare without impiety
To challenge heavenly aid, and swell the breast

With confidence of more than mortal vigour,
Can Heaven stand neuter in a cause like this?
Or favour fraud, oppression, cruelty?
—Now gentle friends I am a suitress to you.

ALMADA
You are our sovereign, madam—'tis your right,
Not to solicit but command our duty.

DUTCHESS
Think me not light, capricious, variable,
If I who urg'd ye to this bold attempt,
And ever when your anger seem'd to cool
Pour'd oil to wake the flame and feed its blaze,
Now supplicate with milder earnestness
And strive to allay its fury.

ALMADA
Speak your pleasure!
The obedience of our hearts will follow it!

DUTCHESS
I know the measure of your wrongs would license,
Nay justify the wild excess of vengeance;
Yet in the headlong rage of execution,
Think rather what your mercy may permit
Than what their crimes deserve who feel your justice.
O! follow not the example we abhor,
Nor let those weapons justice consecrates
Be dy'd with drops drawn from the bleeding breast
Of reverend age, or helpless innocence.
Wilt thou take heed Almada?

ALMADA
Fear not, madam,
All mercy not injurious to our cause,
Ev'n Spaniards, as they are men, from men may challenge.
For Indus' wealth I wou'd not stain this sword,
Sacred to honour, in the guiltless blood
Of unoffending wretches—rest secure,
A prostrate and defenceless enemy,
Has stronger guards against a brave man's wrath,
Than tenfold brass, or shields of adamant.

DUTCHESS
Gen'rous Almada! well dost thou instruct—
Soft pity is not more akin to love
Than to true fortitude.—Thy soft youth, Mendoza,

Need not be tutor'd to humanity.

MENDOZA
Heav'n and my conscious soul bear witness for me,
That not to satiate any private malice,
But for the general good, I stand engag'd
In this great compact.—'Twere a coward's vengeance
To turn a sacrifice to massacre.
And practice while I punish cruelty.

RIBIRO
Till fortune give one victim to my rage,
Compassion and this bosom must be strangers,
No sanctuary, nor interceding prayers,
Nor wings of angels stretch'd to cover him,
Shall save that monster from the doom he merits.

DUTCHESS
You mean the minister of Spain, Velasquez.

RIBIRO
I mean the minister of hell, Velasquez,
That cool deliberate executioner;
If he escape, may this good arm rot off,
All worthy thoughts forsake, and scorn pursue me:
Write boaster on my forehead—let my name
Blister the tongue that speaks it.—Infamy
Be here my portion, endless pains hereafter.

DUTCHESS
O would that sacrifice might expiate!—

RIBIRO
Pardon the rash effusion of my zeal;
It deals too much in words.

DUTCHESS
Not so, Ribiro,
Thy anger has a license;—and thy zeal
We know is generous, not sanguinary.

ALMADA
Madam, we take our leave—good angels guard you!
We go to prove our duty in your service.
The homage of our hearts has long been yours,
And soon you shall receive it from our knees.

DUTCHESS

Believe me, friends, your loves are written here,
In characters no time can e'er efface.

[Exeunt **ALMADA**, **RIBIRO** and **MENDOZA**.

DUTCHESS [Alone]
And may the mighty spirits of past times
Rais'd by desert to bright immortal thrones,
Suspend awhile their task of heav'nly praise
In ministry unseen to hover round them!
Protect aspiring virtue like their own,
And in their bosoms breathe resistless ardour!

[Exit.

ACT III

SCENE I

The Apartments of Velasquez, in the Palace of the Vice-Queen

VELASQUEZ, PIZARRO.

PIZARRO
You seem disturb'd—

VELASQUEZ
With reason—dull Braganza
Must have been tutor'd—At our interview
I practis'd every supple artifice
That glides into man's bosom—The return
Was blank reserve, ambiguous compliment,
And hatred thinly veil'd by ceremony.

PIZARRO
Might I presume—

VELASQUEZ
Pizarro, I am stung—
His father Theodosius, that proud Prince,
Who durst avow his enmity to Philip,
And menac'd thunders at my destin'd head,
With all his empty turbulence of rage
Cou'd never move me like the calm disdain
Of this cold blooded Juan.

PIZARRO
Then, my Lord,
Your purpose holds.

VELASQUEZ
It does—I will dispatch
This tow'ring Duke, who keeps the cheek of Spain
Pale with perpetual danger.

PIZARRO
For what end?
Unconscious of his fate, he blindly speeds
To find a grave in Spain—Why then resolve
To spill that blood, which elsewhere will be shed
Without your crime or peril?

VELASQUEZ
That's the question.
Were I assur'd they meant his death, 'twere needless:
But when they draw him once from Portugal,
Where only he is dangerous, then perhaps
Their fears, or lenity may let him live;
And while he lives, my fiery course is check'd,
My sun climbs slowly, never can ascend
To its meridian brightness.

PIZARRO
Still, my Lord,
My short lin'd wisdom cannot sound your depth.

VELASQUEZ
I mean to tell thee all, for thou may'st aid me,
And thy tried faith deserves my confidence.

PIZARRO
I am your own for ever—Your kind hand,
Bounteous beyond my merit, planted here
Favours innumerable. —

VELASQUEZ
—Think them little—
An earnest, not the acquittal of my love.
The enormous wealth of Juan's royal house,
His large domains, extended influence,
His numerous vassals so have swell'd his state,
That were his means but push'd to one great end;
How easy might he wrest this realm from Spain,
And brave King Philip's rage?

PIZARRO

Good careless prince!
Mild and uxorious! No ambitious dream
Disturbs his tranquil slumber —

VELASQUEZ

Just his nature!
On household wing he flutters round the roof,
That with the princely eagle might have soar'd
And met the dazzling sun. Now by his death
(My engine cannot fail, this night he meets it)
His wealth, his mightiness, his followers
Become Louisa's dower—What think'st thou now?
Cou'd I but win her to accept my hand,
(And much my art will move, and more my power)
Might not our union, like the impetuous course
Of blending torrents, break all feeble mounds
Spain cou'd oppose to bar me from the crown?
That once obtain'd, let Olivarez rail,
Let his inglorious master call me traitor,
I'll scorn their idle fury.

PIZARRO

Still I fear
Louisa's heart, cold and impenetrable,
To all but Juan's love, will own no second,
Tho' big ambition swells her female breast
Beyond the sex's softness.

VELASQUEZ

My hope rests
Even on that favourite passion—Grief at first
Will drive her far from love— A second flame
Perhaps may ne'er rekindle in her heart;
Yet, give her momentary frenzy scope,
It wastes itself; ambition then regains
Its wonted force and winds her to my lure—
But come—I must not lose these precious moments,
The Fates are busy now—What's yet untold,
There place thyself and learn—Take heed you move not.

[**PIZARRO** retires.

Without there! Ho!

[Enter an **OFFICER**

OFFICER
What is your lordship's pleasure?

VELASQUEZ
Attends the monk, Ramirez?

OFFICER
He does, my lord.

VELASQUEZ
Conduct him in and leave us.

[Enter **RAMIREZ**.

You are welcome,
Most welcome, reverend father—Pray draw near—
We have a business for your privacy,
Of an especial nature—The circling air
Shou'd not partake it, nor the babbling winds,
Lest their invisible wings disperse one breath
Of that main secret, which thy faithful bosom
Is only fit to treasure.

RAMIREZ
Good my lord,
I am no common talker.

VELASQUEZ
Well I know it,
And therefore chose thee from the brotherhood,
Not one of whom but wou'd lay by all thoughts
Of earth and Heaven, and fly to execute
What I, the voice of Spain, commission'd him.

RAMIREZ
Vouchsafe directly to unfold your will,
My deeds, and not my words, must prove my duty.

VELASQUEZ
Nay, trust me, cou'd they but divine my purpose,
The holiest he, that wastes the midnight lamp
In prayers and penance, wou'd prevent my tongue
And hear me thank the deed, but not persuade it.
Therefore, good friend, 'tis not necessity,
That sometimes forces any present means,
And chequers chance with wisdom, but free will,
The election of my judgment and my love,
That gives thy aptness this pre-eminence.

RAMIREZ

The state, I know, has store of instruments,
Like well-rang'd arms in ready order plac'd,
Each for its several use.

VELASQUEZ

Observe me well;
Think not I mean to snatch a thankless office;
Who serves the state, while I direct her helm,
Commands my friendship, and his own reward.
Say, can you be content in these poor weeds
To know no earthly hopes beyond a cloyster?
But stretch'd on musty matts in noisome caves,
To rouse at midnight bells, and mutter prayers
For souls beyond their reach, to senseless saints?
To wage perpetual war with nature's bounty?
To blacken sick men's chambers, and be number'd
With the loath'd leavings of mortality,
The watch-light, hour-glass, and the nauseous phial?
Are these the ends of life? Was this fine frame,
Nerves exquisitely textur'd, soft desires,
Aspiring thoughts, this comprehensive soul,
With all her train of god-like faculties
Given to be sunk in this vile drudgery?

RAMIREZ

These are the hard conditions of our state.
We sow our humble seeds with toil on earth,
To reap the harvest of our hopes in Heaven.

VELASQUEZ

Yet wiser they who trust no future chance,
But make this earth a Heaven. Raise thy eyes
Up to the temporal splendors of our church;
Behold our priors, prelates, cardinals;
Survey their large revenues, princely state,
Their palaces of marble, beds of down,
Their statues, pictures, baths, luxurious tables,
That shame the fabled banquets of the gods.
See how they weary art, and ransack nature
To leave no taste, no wish ungratified.
Now—if thy spirit shrink not—I can raise thee
To all this pomp and greatness.—Pledge thy faith,
Swear thou wil't do this thing—whate'er I urge,
—And Lisbon's envied crozier shall be thine,

RAMIREZ

This goodness, so transcending all my hopes,
Confounds my astonish'd sense.—Whate'er it be
Within the compass of man's power to act,
I here devote me to the execution.

VELASQUEZ
I must not hear of conscience and nice scruples,
Tares that abound in none but meagre soils,
To choak the aspiring seeds of manly daring:
Those puny instincts, which in feeble minds,
Unfit for great exploits, are miscall'd virtue—

RAMIREZ
Still am I lost in dark uncertainty;
And must for ever wander, till thy breath
Deign to dispel the impenetrable mist,
Fooling my sight that strives in vain to pierce it.

VELASQUEZ
You are the Duke of Braganza's confessor,
And fame reports him an exact observer
Of all our churches' holy ceremonies.
He still is won't whene'er he visits Lisbon,
Ere grateful slumber seal his pious lids,
With all due reverence, from some priestly hand
To take the mystic symbol of our faith.

RAMIREZ
It ever was his custom, and this night
I am commanded to attend his leisure
With preparation for the solemn act.

VELASQUEZ
I know it—Take—
[Gives him a box]
—thou this—It holds a wafer
Of sovereign virtue to enfranchise souls,
Too righteous for this world, from mortal cares.
A monk of Milan mix'd the deadly drug,
Drawn from the quintessence of noxious plants,
Minerals and poisonous creatures, whose dull bane
Arrests the nimble current of life's tide,
And kills without a pang.

RAMIREZ
I knew him well,
The Carmelite Castruccio, was it not?

VELASQUEZ

The same, he first approv'd it on a wretch
Condemn'd for murder to the ling'ring wheel.
This night commit it to Braganza's lips.
Had he a heart of iron, giant strength,
The antidotes of Pontus—All were vain,
To struggle with the venom's potency.

RAMIREZ

This night, my lord?

VELASQUEZ

This very night, nay, shrink not,
Unless thou mean'st to take the lead in death,
And pull thy own destruction on thy head.

RAMIREZ

Give me a moment's pause—A deed like this—

VELASQUEZ

Should be at once resolv'd and executed.
Think'st thou I am a raw unpractis'd novice,
To make thy breast a partner to the trust,
And not thy hand accomplice of the crime?
Why 'tis the bond for my security:
Look not amaz'd, but mark me heedfully.
Thou hast thy choice—dispatch mine enemy.
The means are in thy hand—be safe and great,
Or instantly prepare thee for a death
Which nothing but compliance can avert.

RAMIREZ

Numbers I know even thus have tasted death,
But sure imagination scarce can form
A way so horrid, impious!

VELASQUEZ

How's this, How's this!
Hear me, pale miscreant, my rage once rous'd,
That hell thou dread'st this moment shall receive thee.
Look here and tremble— Draws a dagger and seizes him.

RAMIREZ

My lord be not so rash,
Your fury's deaf—Will you not hear me speak?
By ev'ry hope that cheers, all vows that bind,
Whatever horror waits upon the act,
Your will shall make it justice—I'm resolv'd.

VELASQUEZ
No trifling, Monk—take heed, for should'st thou fail—

RAMIREZ
Then be my life the forfeit—My obedience
Not only follows from your high command,
But that my bosom swells against this Duke
With the full sense of my own injuries.—

VELASQUEZ
Enough—I thank thee—Let me know betimes
How we have prosper'd. Hence, retire with caution,
Deserve my favour, and then meet me boldly. Exit Ramirez.
'Tis done—His doom is seal'd—Come forth Pizarro.
Pizarro comes forward.
Is't not a subtle mischief?

PIZARRO
Past all praise,
The holy tool had qualms.

VELASQUEZ [Pointing to his dagger]
But this dispell'd them,
And fortified the coward by his fears.
His work perform'd, I mean to end him too. —
Say, is my barge prepar'd as I commanded?

PIZARRO
All is prepar'd, my Lord.

VELASQUEZ
The friends of Juan,
(I'll tell thee as we pass) they shall not long
Survive to lift their crests so high in Lisbon.

[Exeunt.

SCENE changes to the Castle of Almada

Enter **ALMADA** and an **ATTENDANT**.

ALMADA
Good Perez, see that none to night have entrance
But such whose names are written in that roll,
And bid your fellows from the northern tower,

Chuse each a faulchion, and prepare to follow
Where I at dawn will lead.

ATTENDANT
I will, my Lord.

ALMADA
Wait near the gate thyself, nor stir from thence
Without my summons.

ATTENDANT
Trust my vigilance.

[Exit **ATTENDANT**.

ALMADA [Alone]
Now rayless midnight flings her sable pall
Athwart the horizon, and with pond'rous mace
In dead repose weighs down o'er-labour'd nature,
While we, the busy instruments of fate,
Unmindful of her season, wake like ghosts,
To add new horrors to the shadowy scene.

[To him enter several of the Duke of Braganza's **FRIENDS**.

ANTONIO
Health to Almada.

ALMADA
Thus to meet, Antonio!
Is the best health, the soundness of the mind.
Better at this dark hour to embrace in arms
Thus girt for manly execution, friend!
Than in the mazes of the wanton dance,
Or revelling o'er bowls in frantic mirth,
To keep inglorious vigils.

ANTONIO.
True, my Lord.

[Enter **RIBIRO** with **LEMOS** and **COREA**.

ALMADA [To **RIBIRO**]
O soul of honour, ever, ever constant.
These are the worthy citizens, our friends—

RIBIRO [Presenting **LEMOS** and **COREA**]
And such as laurell'd Rome might well have own'd

Worthy to fill her magisterial chairs,
When reverence bow'd to virtue tho' untitled.

ALMADA
As such I take their hands, nay more as such,
Their grateful country will rejoice to own them.
Are we all met?

ANTONIO
Mendoza is not here,
Nor Roderic, and Mello too is absent.

ALMADA
They were not wont to be thus waited for.

RIBIRO
Anon they will be here,—mean time proceed,
They know their place already —

ALMADA
Why we meet,
Is not to canvass our opprobrious wrongs,
But to redress them.—Yet as trumpets sound,
To rouse the soldier's ardor,—so the breath
Of our calamities will wake our fires,
And fan them to spread wide the flame of vengeance.
'Tis not my gift to play the orator,
But in plain words to lay our state before you.
—Our tyrant's grandsire, whose ambition claim'd,
And first usurp'd Braganza's royal rights,
My blood establish'd his detested sway.
Old Tagus blush'd with many a crimson tide,
Sluic'd from the noblest veins of Portugal.
The exterminating sword knew no distinction.
Princes, and prelates, venerable age,
Matrons, and helpless virgins fell together,
'Till cloy'd and sick of slaughter, the tir'd soldier
With grim content flung down his reeking steel,
And glutted rage gave truce to massacre.

RIBIRO
Nor pass'd the iron rod to milder hands
Thro' two succeeding reigns—With cruel zeal
The barbarous offspring emulate their sire,
And track his bloody footsteps in our ruin.

ALMADA
Now mark how happily the time conspires,

To give our great atchievement permanence;
—Spain is not what she was, when Europe bow'd
To the fifth Charles, and his degenerate son.
When, like a torrent swell'd by mountain floods,
She swept the neighbouring nations with her arms,
And threaten'd those remote,—contracted now
Within an humble bed, the thrifty urn,
Of her exhausted greatness, scarce can pour
A lazy tide thro' her own mould'ring states.

RIBIRO
Yes the Colossus totters, every blast
Shakes the stupendous mass and threats its downfall.

[Enter **MENDOZA.**

MENDOZA
Break off—break off—the fatal snare is spread,
And death's pale hand assists to close the toil.

ALMADA
Whence this dread greeting?—Ha—thy alter'd cheek
Wears not the ensign of this glowing hour.

MENDOZA
The scream of night owls, or the ravens croak
Wou'd better suit the baleful news I bring,
Than the known accents of a friendly voice.
—We are undone—betray'd—

ALMADA
Say'st thou—betray'd?

MENDOZA
Our tower is sap'd—the high rais'd fabric falls
To crush us with the ruin.—What avails
The full maturity of all our hopes?
This glorious league—the justice of our cause?—
—High Heaven might idly thunder on our side,
If traitors to ourselves.—

ALMADA
Ourselves—Oh shame!
I'll not believe it — What perfidious slaves—

MENDOZA
Two whom we thought the sinews of our strength,
Don Roderic and Mello.—

RIBIRO

Lightnings blast them!
May infamy record their dastard names,
And vulgar villains shun their fellowship—
These hot, loud brawlers—

MENDOZA

Are the slaves of Spain,
And bargain for the price of perfidy.—
On to the wharf with quick impatient step,
I saw Velasquez press, and in his train
These lurking traitors.—Now, even now, they cross
The ebbing Tagus in the tyrant's barge,
And hasten to the sort.—The troops of Spain,
Even while we speak, are summon'd to the charge,
And mark us for their prey.

ALMADA

Nay then, 'tis past.
Malignant fortune, when the cup was rais'd
Close to our lips, has dash'd it to the ground.

RIBIRO

This unexpected bolt strikes flat our hopes,
And leaves one dreary desolation round us.
I see their hangmen muster—wolf-ey'd cruelty,
Grimly sedate, glares o'er her iron hoard
Of racks, wheels, engines, feels her axe's edge
Licks her fell jaws, and with a monster's thirst,
Already drinks our blood.

MENDOZA

There's not a pang
That rends the fibres of man's feeling frame,
No vile disgrace, that even in thought o'er-spreads
The cheek with burning crimson, but her hate
Ingenious to devise, and sure to inflict
In keenest agony will make us suffer.

ALMADA

Wou'd that were all—Our dismal scene must close;
Nature o'er power'd at length will leave her load,
And baffie persecution.—But O, Portugal!
Alass unhappy country! Where's the bourn
Can mark the extent of thy calamities.
Like winter's icy hand our luckless end
Will freeze the source of future enterprize:

Oppression then o'er the devoted realm
Erect and bold will stalk with tenfold ravage.
There, there alone, this breast is vulnerable;
These are the wheels that wrench, the racks that tear me.

ANTONIO

But are there left no means to elude the danger?
Why do we linger here?—Why not resolve
To save ourselves by flight?

MENDOZA

Impossible!
The guards no doubt are set—the port is bar'd.

ALMADA

Fly Lemos to the people, and restrain
Their generous ardor.—It wou'd now break forth
Useless to us, and fatal to themselves. Exit Lemor.
You to the Duke, Ribiro!—In our names,
(Perhaps our last request) by our lost fortunes,
By all our former friendship, O conjure him
To save our richest treasure from the wreck,
Nor hazard in a desperate enterprize
His country's last best hope, his valued life.

RIBIRO

Support him Heaven, and arm his piety
To bear this sad vicissitude with patience. Exit Ribiro.

ALMADA

And yet we will not meet in vain, brave friends;
We came with better hopes, resolv'd like men
To struggle for our freedom.—What remains?
A greater power than mortals can arraign,
Has otherwise decreed it.—Speak, my brothers,
Now doubly dear in stern adversity;
Say, shall we glut the spoiler with our blood,
Submit to the vile insults of their law,
To have our honest dust by the ruffian hands
Given to the winds—Is this the doom that waits us?

MENDOZA

Alas what better doom? To ask for mercy
Were ignominious, to expect it bootless.

ALMADA

To ask for mercy—cou'd Spain stretch my life
To years beyond the telling, for one tear,

One word, in sign of sorrow, I'd disdain it.
Death still is in our pow'r—and we'll die nobly,
As soldiers shou'd do, red with well earn'd wounds,
And stretch'd on heaps of slaughter'd enemies.

[Exeunt **SEVERALLY**.

ACT IV

SCENE I

A Chamber in the Duke of Braganza's Palace

DUTCHESS [Alone]
O Thou supreme disposer of the world!
If from my childhood to this awful now,
I've bent with meek submission to thy will,
Send to this feeble bosom one blest beam
Of that bright emanation, which inspires
True confidence in thee, to calm the throbs
That heave this bosom for my husband's safety,
And with immortal spirit to exalt
Above all partial ties our countries love.

[To her enter **RIBIRO** hastily.

RIBIRO
Where is the Duke? O pardon, gracious madam.

DUTCHESS
What means this haste and these distracted looks?

RIBIRO
Detain me not—but lead me to my Lord.—
His life, perhaps—nay, your—

DUTCHESS
His life—O heavens!
Tell me, Ribiro—speak—

RIBIRO
Too soon, alas
You'll hear it—Ask not now dear lady
What I've scarce breath to utter—Where's the Duke?

DUTCHESS

This moment with his confessor retir'd
I left him in his closet.

RIBIRO
—'Tis no time—
All must give place to this dire urgency.
Even while we speak—A moment's precious now.—
He must be interrupted—Guide me to him.

DUTCHESS
Suspense is ling'ring death.—Come on, I'll lead you.

[Exeunt.

[Enter **RAMIREZ.**

RAMIREZ
O welcome interruption—Pitying Heaven
A while at least arrests the murd'rous deed,
And gives a moment's respite from damnation.
—Is there a hell beyond this war of conscience?
My blood runs backward, and my tottering knees
Refuse to bear their sacrilegious load.
Methought the statues of his ancestors,
As I pass'd by them, shook their marble heads;
His father's picture seem'd to frown in wrath,
And its eye pierce me, while I trembling stood
Assassin like before it—Hush—I'm summon'd.

[Re-enter **DUTCHESS.**

DUTCHESS
Get you to rest good father—Fare you well.
Some unexpected business of the state
Demands my Lord's attention—For this night
Your holy function must be unperform'd
Till more convenient season.

RAMIREZ
Holy function! aside.
I humbly take my leave, and will not fail
To recommend you in my prayers to Heaven.

[Exit **RAMIREZ**.

DUTCHESS
The Heavens I fear are shut and will not hear them.
—Now gush my tears—now break at once my heart!

While in my Juan's presence, I suppress'd
The bursting grief—But here give nature way!
Is there a hope—Oh no—All horrible—
My children too—Their little lives—My husband—
I conquer'd his reluctance—I persuaded
By every power his boundless passion gave me—
I thought it virtue too—Mysterious Heaven?—
Then I, and only I, have work'd his ruin.

[Enter **DUKE.**

DUKE
Alas my love, why must thy Juan seek thee?
Why do'st thou shun me at this aweful moment?
The few sad hours our destiny permits,
Shou'd sure be spent together.

DUTCHESS
Must we part then?

DUKE
I fear we must for ever in this world,
Till that great power who fashion'd us in life,
Unites us once again no more to fever;
In those blest regions of eternal peace,
Where sorrow never enters, where thy truth,
Thy unexampl'd fortitude and sweetness,
Will meet their full reward.

DUTCHESS
Where is the friend
Who rung our dismal knell?

DUKE
Good, generous man!
Assur'd of death, yet careless of his life,
And anxious but for us, he is return'd,
To know what our brave leaders will determine—
Yet what can they determine but to die?
Our numbers poorly arm'd, undisciplin'd,
May fight and fall with desperate obstinacy,
For valour can no more—But, oh Louisa!
Friends, country, life itself, all lost seem little;
One sharp devouring grief consumes the rest,
And makes thee all its object.

DUTCHESS
My dear husband!

These soft endearments, this excess of fondness,
Strike deeper to my soul, than all the pangs
The subtlest vengeance cou'd contrive to wound me.
Oh fly me, hate me, call me murderess;
'Tis I have driven thee to this precipice,
I urge the ruffian hand of law to seize thee,
I drag thee to the block,—I lift the axe,
(Oh agony) Louisa dooms thee dead!

DUKE
—'Tis anguish insupportable to hear thee
Add self-upbraidings to our misery.
Thou my destroyer! No my best Louisa,
Thou art my guardian angel.—At this hour,
This dreadful hour, 'tis safety to be near thee.
Those dastards who betray'd our brave design,
That baseness which no caution cou'd prevent,
Nor wisdom cou'd foresee, 'twas that undid us.
I will not curse them—Yet I swear by honour,
Thus hunted to the utmost verge of fate,
Without one ray of hope to cheer the danger,
I wou'd not barter this dire certainty,
For that ignoble life those bad men purchase
By perfidy and vileness—

DUTCHESS
Oh two such—
But indignation wants a tongue to name them.
How was their fury thunder'd on our side!
Their youthful veins full of Patrician blood
Insulted by Velasquez—stript by Spain
Of all the ancient honours of their house;
Sworn at the altar to assert this cause
By holiest adjurations:—Yet these two
To turn apostates—Can this fleeting breath,
This transitory, frail, uncertain being,
Be worth so vast a ransom?

DUKE
Yes, to cowards,
Such ever be the proselytes of Spain,—
Leave them to scorn.—Fain wou'd I turn my thoughts
From this bad world—shake off the clogs of earth,
And for that great tribunal, arm my soul,
Where Heaven, not Spain, must judge me—but in vain;
My soften'd mind still hangs on those blest days,
Those years of sweet tranquility and peace,
When smiling morn but wak'd us to new joys,

And love at night shed blessings on our pillow.

DUTCHESS
These hours are fled, and never can return.
'Tis Heaven's high will, and be that will obeyed.
The retrospect of past felicity
Plucks not the barbed arrow from the wound,
But makes it rankle deeper.—Come my Juan,
Here bid adieu to this infectious grief,
Let's knit our constancy to meet the trial;
Shall we be bold in words, mere moral talkers?
Declaim with pedant tongue in virtue's praise,
Yet find no comfort, no support within
From her bright energy? — It comes—it comes,
I feel my breast dilate—The phantom, death,
Shrinks at the radiant vision—bright ey'd hope
Bids us aspire, and points the shining throne.—
—Spain, I defy thee!

DUKE
O would she hew the elm,
And spare the tender vine—This stubborn trunk
Shou'd brave her fury. Here is royal blood,
And blood long thirsted for.—They cannot dare,
Insatiate as they are, remorseless, savage,
With sacrilegious hands to violate
This beauteous sanctuary.—Let me not think.
Distraction—horror—Oh it splits my brain,
Rends every vital string, and tears my heart.
Mercy can grant no more—nor I petition,
Than to fall dead this instant and forget it.
I look towards Heaven in vain.—Gape wide, O earth,
And bury, bury deep this load of anguish.

DUTCHESS
Be not so lost.—Hear, Oh hear me Juan,
My lord, my life, my love.—Wilt thou not speak?
He heeds me not.—What shall I say to move him?
For pity's sake look up.—Oh think Braganza,
Cou'd Spain behold thee thus—

DUKE
Oh no, Louisa,
No eye shall see me melt.—I will be calm,
Still, silent, motionless.—Oh tough, tough heart,
Wou'd I could weep to ease thee—

DUTCHESS

Here, weep here,
Pour the warm stream into this faithful breast,
Thy sorrows here shall find a kindred source,
Which flows for every tear with drops of blood.
Now summon all thy soul.—Behold, he comes
To thunder our irrevocable doom.

[Enter **RIBIRO.**

RIBIRO
O for an angel's organ to proclaim
Such gratulations as no tongue can speak,
Nor mortal breast conceive—joy, boundless joy.

DUKE
Am I awake?—Thou can'st not mean to mock me.

RIBIRO
I shall go wild with transport.—On my knee
I beg you to forgive the cruel shock
This tongue (Heaven knows with what severe reluctance)
So lately gave to all your dearest hopes.

DUKE
No, let me take that posture: for I swear,
Tho' yet I know not why, my lighten'd heart
Beats freer, and seems eas'd of half its burthen.
—Forgive my strong impatience—quickly tell me.

RIBIRO
Still ignorant of our intended vengeance,
Velasquez is return'd.—Our gallant friends
Were wrong'd by rash suspicion.—

DUKE
Heard I right?
Or is't illusion all? (embracing him) Thus let me thank thee.
Louisa then is safe—Fountain of mercy!
These late despairing arms again enfold her,
My Queen, my love, my wife!—

DUTCHESS
Flow, flow my tears;
Take, bounteous lord of all, this melting tribute,
My heart can give no more for all thy goodness.

DUKE
And now disclose this wonder.

RIBIRO

Thus, my lord,
When at the appointed time, our two brave friends
Were hast'ning to Almada, near the square,
Velasquez and his followers cross'd their steps,
Their course seem'd towards the river;—struck with fear,
And ignorant what cause at that late hour
Cou'd draw him from the palace; straight they chang'd
Their first intent of joining our assembly,
And unobserv'd pursu'd the attending train.
Think what these brave men suffer'd when they saw
The tyrant climb his barge, and push from shore.
Their swords were half unsheath'd, both half resolv'd
To rush at once, and pierce him to the heart.
—But prudence, or our fortune check'd their hands.

DUKE

It had been certain ruin—but go on—

RIBIRO

An instant pass'd in thought, they seiz'd a boat,
And following, anxious hung on all his motions:
Mendoza saw them thus—then hurrying back,
Fill'd us with consternation at the tidings.

DUTCHESS

Nor was it strange—it wore a dreadful aspect;
But fear interprets all things to its danger.

RIBIRO

He cross'd the river where Jago's fort
Commands the narrowing stream. The governor
Attended at the gate, a while there pass'd
In short but earnest converse, they took leave,
With hasty strides Velasquez reimbark'd;
The vessel, to the shore she left, return'd,
And her proud master sought again the palace.

DUTCHESS

Cou'd not our valiant friends discover ought
That might reveal his purpose?

RIBIRO

Madam—No.
To have enquir'd too near were dangerous
Besides, their haste to reassure our hopes
Press'd their return—But thus we may resolve:

He apprehends some danger imminent.
He sees above his head the gathering cloud,
But knows not when 'twill burst in thunder on him.

DUKE
Thanks, gentle friend—Alas, I tremble still;
As just escap'd from shipwreck, I look round,
And tho' I tread on earth,—firm, solid earth
See with broad eye the threatning surge far off,
Scarce can I credit my conflicting sense
Or trust our preservation—

DUTCHESS
Thy glad tale
Has rais'd me from the gulph of black despair,
Even to the topmost pinnacle of joy.
Yes, we shall conquer— All these dangers past
Will serve but to enrich the future story.
Our children's children shall recount each fear,
And from the mingled texture of our lives,
Learn to revere that sacred Providence
That guides the strife of virtue.

DUKE
O Louisa!
I thought I knew the extent of all my fondness,
That long acquaintance with thy wondrous virtue
Had given thee such dominion o'er my soul,
Time cou'd not add to my trascendent passion.
But when the danger came, it wak'd new fires,
Presented thee in softer loveliness,
And twin'd thee closer here.

RIBIRO
My Lord, ere this
Our friends expect me.—

DUKE
Let us fly to meet them.
I long to pour into their generous breasts
My cordial greeting.

DUTCHESS
Go my dearest Juan,
To them and all commend me; such rare zeal
Merits more recompence than our poor thanks
Can at the best requite. For souls like theirs
Ill brook the indignity of soul surmise;

And virtue wrong'd demands a double homage.

[Exit **DUTCHESS**.

DUKE
If the good augury of my breast deceive not,
No more such terrors will appal our souls,
But guilt alone shall tremble—Come, Ribiro.

[Exeunt.

SCENE changes to the Castle of Almada

ALMADA and **SEVERAL CONSPIRATORS** as before, with **MELLO** and **RODERIC**.

ALMADA
Again our hopes revive—The unloaded stem
Shakes the wet tempest from its vigorous head,
And rears the swelling harvest to our sight.

MENDOZA
After the chillings of this aguish fear,
Methinks I breathe more free—the vital stream
In sprightlier tides flows through its wonted course,
Warms my whole frame and doubly man's my heart.

ALMADA
And may the generous ardor spread to all—
Observe me friends,—our numbers must divide
Into four equal bands, all to attack
At the bell's signal the four palace gates.
So every passage barr'd, the foe in vain
May strive to unite and overwhelm our force.
Myself with the brave few, who have sworn to follow,
Will rush impetuous on the German guard,
Who at the northern entrance hold their station.
—The fort be Roderic and Mello's care,
With Ferdinand, Henriquez, and Antonio.
—Mendoza, Carlos, and their gallant troop
Must seize the regent Margaret, and secure
The counsellors of Spain as hostages
For the surrender of the citadel.

MENDOZA
Letters to every province are dispers'd
Importing this great change, and all are ready

To shake to earth the intolerable yoke.
Nay distant India, in her sultry mines
Shall hear the chearful sound of liberty;
Again fair commerce welcom'd to our shore,
Shall loose her swelling canvas to the winds,
And golden Tagus heave once more to meet her.
But see the Duke. —

[Enter **DUKE.**

ALMADA
Your unexpected presence,
Like a propitious omen cheers the night,
And gives a royal sanction to this meeting.

DUKE
My wish surpass'd my speed —A call like this
Might imp the tardiness of feeble age.
The general perseverance in our cause
Transcends all gratitude—but these wrong'd virtues—
To Mello and Roderic.

MELLO
Pray forbear;
The painful error brought its punishment.
Ribiro bore our duties to your grace.

DUKE
He did, and soon will join us—On our way
He left me with design once more to view
The posture of the guards,—for still we fear
Some dark impending mischief from Velasquez.

ALMADA
Whatever fortune waits upon our swords,
Your highness must not share the common hazard;
Lest in the tumult some inglorious chance
Deprive your country of its last best bulwark.

DUKE
And shou'd I merit to be call'd her bulwark,
Or rank with men like you.—cou'd I submit
To hear, and not partake the glorious danger?

ALMADA
Pray be advis'd—in this I must command.

DUKE

Then be it so—but yet shou'd ought betide
To claim the interest of thy prince's arm,
I cannot wrong our friendship to suspect
You will forbear my summons to the field.

ALMADA
Trust your Almada—Lo! the night wears fast;
Nor are our scatter'd numbers yet return'd.

DUKE
Welcome Ribiro! What intelligence?

[Enter **RIBIRO.**

RIBIRO
The worst if we delay—Oh had your eyes
Beheld the sight that blasted mine.

DUKE
What fight?

RIBIRO
Lemos is seiz'd this moment—and Pizarro,
The ready tool of fell Velasquez' crimes,
Leads him to prison.

DUKE
Soon we'll wrench the gates,
And from their gloomy caverns draw to light
All that remains of those unhappy men,
Whom unarraign'd unheard the tyrants nod
Consign'd to horrors nature shakes to think of.

ALMADA
His triumph will be short—The subtle fiend
May league with hell to thwart us—but in vain;
His fate or ours must quickly be decided.

RIBIRO
Even now it seems his demon whispers him
His audit is at hand and scares his soul.
Anxious at this late hour, he walks his chamber,
Nor seeks the season's rest—and still more strange
The palace guards stretch'd by their glimmering fires,
Their arms cast by, lye wrapt in thoughtless sleep,

DUKE
Anon we'll rouse them with so loud a peal,

That death's dull ear shall hear it.

ALMADA
Corea!
Soon as our work begins, your hardy tribes
Must thro' the streets proclaim Don Juan King.
Press towards the palace; shou'd our friends give ground,
Sustain their fainting strength.

COREA
We will not fail.

ALMADA
The general suffrage to thy sword, Ribiro,
Commits our master work; a deed so envied
That ev'ry trenchant steel of Portugal
(Did not thy gallant zeal demand it first)
Would strike to share the glory.

RIBIRO [Pointing to his sword]
This shall thank you,
And if it reek not with his hated blood
Exchange it for a distaff.

ALMADA
Friends, I mean not
By gloomy presage to allay your ardor.
We must not look to fortune in this cause:
But on ourselves rely for sure success.
The least disorder in our bold approach,
The least repulse may drive our engine back.
One brave man's rashness, or one coward's fear,
Turns all our fairest hopes to shame and ruin.

DUKE
Now to our stations—Yet ere we depart
This honest pledge, the soldier's short embrace.
The sweet remembrance, if we fall for freedom,
Will more than soften half the pains of dying;
But if we meet, in stronger clasps renew'd,
Will double all the joys of victory.

ACT V

SCENE I

VELASQUEZ [Alone]
Why am I haunted by these phantom fears?
It cannot be my fate. 'Tis nature's weakness:
The spirits rais'd too high, like billows puff'd
By sudden storms, lift up our little bark,
Then slipping from their burthen, sink as fast,
And leave it wreck'd and found'ring.

[Enter **PIZARRO.**

VELASQUEZ
Have you, as I commanded, question'd Lemos?

PIZARRO
Just now I left him.

VELASQUEZ
Has the slave confess'd?

PIZARRO
With sullen calmness he defies your power,
Or answers but with scorn.

VELASQUEZ
We'll find the means
To make him speak more plainly, to bring down
This daring spirit—He is dangerous;
And under the fair mask of public virtue,
Combines with proud Almada and the rest
In dark confed'racy against my state.

PIZARRO
He is, my Lord, the master-spring that moves
The factious populace.

VELASQUEZ
I know it well,
But I have ta'en such care as shall unhinge
Their ill-contriv'd designs. Ere noon to-morrow,
Don Garcia, with the Spanish veterans
From Saint Jago's fortress, shall pour in
And bend these stubborn necks to due obedience.
How will their disappointed fury rave
To find their royal demagogue, Braganza,
The idol their vain worship rais'd so high,
Low levell'd with the earth.—I wonder much

Ramirez not returns—Night's latest watch
Will soon be told.

PIZARRO
Perhaps he but delays
(For better welcome) to behold the effect
Of the dire venom, and to glad your ears
By telling how your enemy expir'd.

VELASQUEZ
It may be so, I cannot doubt the effect;
Poison administer'd will do its work,
And this most speedily; 'tis swift perdition.
Yet, tho' this hour cuts off my greatest foe,
If my firm soul were capable of fear,
I might distrust the promise of my fortunes.

PIZARRO
Wherefore, my Lord?

VELASQUEZ
I almost blush to tell it,
Tir'd with the travail of this anxious night,
I threw me on my couch, and try'd to rest;
I try'd in vain—my vexed lids scarce clos'd;
Or when a momentary slumber seal'd them,
Strange visions swam before their twilight sense:
—But why retrace the hideous phantasy?
Yet still it hovers round me, still remains
A fearful reverence of the past illusion.

PIZARRO
Such reverence but degrades a noble mind,
And sinks its vigour to an infant's weakness.
Beldams and priests infuse these idle fears,
And turn the milk of nature to its bane. Noise at a distance.

VELASQUEZ
Heard you that noise? Didst thou not mark, Pizarro?
The monk has kept his word—'Tis Juan's knell:
His followers who shouted him at noon,
Now wail his death.—My genius now has room;
Their sorrows are my triumph, and proclaim
Assur'd success to my aspiring soul.

PIZARRO
Sure 'tis the din of clashing arms—again—
It comes this way—

[Enter **OFFICER** with his sword drawn.

VELASQUEZ
Ha! bleeding—speak
Know you the cause?—Speak, instant, speak—

OFFICER
Too well!
The raging multitude have forc'd their way;
Their cry is, Where's the tyrant?—Where's Velasquez?
Don Juan's at their head, and guides the storm.

VELASQUEZ
Juan alive! eternal silence seize thee!
Impossible!

OFFICER
These eyes, my Lord, beheld him—
Saw his rais'd arm—

VELASQUEZ
Ha! am I then betray'd!
Perdition catch Ramirez—You, Pizarro,
Collect my scatter'd train—I'll forth, and meet
The rebel's sword.

PIZARRO
Be not so rash,
Nor venture singly—

[Exit **VELASQUEZ.**

OFFICER
He rushes on his death.
Two of my soldiers are already slain,
Striving to bar the outward palace gates;
Where like a tide the frantic people press,
Bearing down all before them.

PIZARRO
Hence, begone;
The uproar's louder—Wake the sleeping grooms—
Bid them bring arms—Alarm the magistrates—
Send to the guard and draw them to the square.

[Exit **OFFICER.**

[Re-enter **VELASQUEZ**.

VELASQUEZ
Ruin'd! undone! all's lost—the streets are throng'd
With raging citizens—A furious band
Of armed Portugueze just now are mounting,
Fate's bloody book is open'd; and I read
My dreadful doom: yet I'll not tamely yield,
But grapple to the last with destiny.

PIZARRO
All is not lost—perhaps some means are left.

VELASQUEZ
Just at the gate I met the dastard monk
Struggling for entrance—scarce his breath suffic'd
To tell me that our purpose had miscarried,
And Juan lives—I stabb'd him to the heart,
The best reward for unperforming fear.

PIZARRO
Think not of him—but save yourself by flight.

VELASQUEZ
Where can I fly?—I am beset, devoted—
Our foes like famish'd blood-hounds are abroad,
And have us in the wind.

PIZARRO
Resolve at once.—
The postern's yet unforc'd, that way escape,
Disguise yourself, and fly to Juan's palace.
'Tis but the terrace length—Implore his mercy;
It is the foolish weakness of his nature
To spare where he may punish.

VELASQUEZ
Ask my life!
No, rather let me perish—Hold—his wife—
Perhaps alone, unguarded—If I fall,
I'll leave a scorpion in the traitor's breast,
Shall make him curse the hour he rous'd my fury.

[Exit

PIZARRO [Alone]
Now let the tempest rise—Oh, fickle fortune!
This moment mounted to thy giddy top,

Now whirl'd to earth and groveling—Hark—they come.

RIBIRO [Entering with **OTHERS**]
Search all the chambers—If the villain 'scape
Our work's but half accomplish'd—

PIZARRO
Pass no farther.

RIBIRO
This is the tyrant's bosom counsellor.
Where is thy master, Spaniard?

PIZARRO
Safe, I hope,
From lawless rage like thine, and still will live
To punish this outrageous violence.

RIBIRO
Insolent slave—And yet I like thy courage.
'Tis vain to strive, deliver up thy sword.
I will not force thee to betray thy master,
Perfidious as he is—Even in a foe
I can discern a virtue, and esteem it.
Gonsalez, guard him safe—the rest disperse,
And leave no place unsearch'd—He must be found:
But by your loves I charge you kill him not.
Rob not my sword, but leave that stroke for me.

[Exeunt severally.

SCENE changes to the Duke of Braganza's Palace

Enter **DUTCHESS**, an **ATTENDANT** following.

DUTCHESS
No, Ines, no, I love my husband much,
But more his honour. Cou'd I press his stay
In tame inaction here to wait the event,
While almost in his sight, his crown and glory
Hung on the doubtful fate of others swords?
Wou'd he have heard me? No, I knew him better.
Soon as Almada's danger reach'd his ear,
Who twice repuls'd cou'd scarce renew the charge,
(Swift as a javelin cuts the whistling air)
He snatch'd his sword, and breaking from my arms,

Rush'd to the fight, and join'd the warring throng.

INES
That favouring power which has so oft preserv'd,
Will not forsake him now.

DUTCHESS
O grant it Heaven!
Go, Ines, to the terrace, and observe
If any friend (for sure I may expect it)
Bring tidings from my husband.

[Exit **INES**.

Would this arm,
This feeble arm had strength to second him!
The conflict here is worse.—My restless heart,
Swell'd with eventful expectation, throbs
And feels its bounds too narrow.—Fear on fear,
Like light reflected from the dancing wave,
Visits all places, but can rest in none.
The distant shouts, that break the morning sky,
Lift up a while my mounting thoughts to Heaven,
Then sinking, leave them to fall down as low,
In boding apprehension.—Welcome, welcome?

[Enter **MENDOZA**.

What of my lord?

MENDOZA
He bad me fly to greet you;
Himself a while detain'd to stop the rage
Of cruelty and carnage.

DUTCHESS
He returns
Unhurt, victorious to these happy arms?

MENDOZA
All, all your fondest wish cou'd form he brings,
Crown, conquest, all.—Oppression is no more,
Pierc'd by a thousand wounds the giant dies,
While free-born men with fearless gaze walk round,
And view the monster's bulk.

DUTCHESS
I wou'd know more.—

Was it a dear bought triumph? Must we mourn
The fall of many friends?

MENDOZA
Scarce one of note
But lives to share our joy.—The regent seiz'd,
Gave orders for the citadel's surrender,
To save the threaten'd lives of the whole council,
Whom sleeping we secur'd.—Poorly content
To obey her mandate, though he knew it forc'd,
The dastard governor resign'd his charge,
And struck the Austrian banner.—Such the power
Of Juan's royal name, and conquering arm.
The rest himself will tell.—I must return.—
Abroad the wild commotion rages still;
The King may want my service—Angels guard you.

[Exit **MENDOZA**.

DUTCHESS
O fly, begone, lose not a thought on me.
Now to thy rest, my soul, thy pray'rs are heard.
From this white hour the bright revolving sun
With kinder beams shall view this smiling land;
A grateful people, by my Juan's arm,
Rescued from shameful bonds, shall bless his name,
And own him their preserver.

[Enter **INES**.

From my lord?

INES
Madam, not yet—A stranger at the gate,
Disguis'd, and almost breathless with his fears,
With earnest importunity entreats
He may have leave to cast him at your feet.
His accents mov'd me much; he seems afflicted.

DUTCHESS
Some wretch escap'd from the pursuer's rage,
And flies for shelter here.—Yes, let him come.

[Exit **INES**.

DUTCHESS [Alone]
Wou'd I cou'd save them all—my woman's soul,
Forc'd from her place in this tumultuous scene.

But ill supports the assum'd severity,
And finds her native seat in soft compassion.

[Enter **VELASQUEZ**, disguised.

Whoe'er thou art, be safe.—The greedy sword
Will have enough of death, and well may spare
One fugitive, who shuns its cruel edge
To wait the stroke of nature.—Trust thy safety.—
Why do thy doubtful eyes so oft look round?
Here are no enemies.—My word is pass'd
Inviolable as recorded oaths.—
—Methinks I have seen that face.—Say, art thou not—

VELASQUEZ
The man you most shou'd fear, most hate.

DUTCHESS
Velasquez!

VELASQUEZ
Yes, that devoted wretch, the lost Velasquez;
From the high top of proud prosperity,
Sunk to this ignominy.

DUTCHESS
Presumptuous man!
If mercy cou'd know bounds, thy monstrous crimes
Almost exceed them.—Speak then, what cou'd urge thee
To seek the shelter of this hostile roof,
And trust a virtue to thy soul a stranger?

VELASQUEZ
Fate left no second choice.—Close at my heels
Revenge and death insatiably pursu'd;
Fear lent me speed, and this way wing'd my flight.
Why flash those eyes with anger?—Royal lady!
Fortune has stripp'd me of the power to injure;
A stingless serpent, a poor fang-drawn lion,
Fitter for scorn than terror.—

DUTCHESS
Thou art fallen!
Yet let me not insult thy alter'd state,
By pity or upbraiding.—If thy life
Be worth the acceptance—take it —and hereafter
Wash out the foulness of thy former deeds
By penitence and better purposes.

[Shouts without.

These joyful sounds proclaim my Juan near
[To **VELASQUEZ**]
—Retire a while till I prepare my lord
To shield thee from the angry nobles rage.
All were combin'd to take thy forfeit life.—

DUKE [Without]
Throw wide the palace gates—Let all have entrance.

DUTCHESS
His well-known voice—'Tis he, 'tis he himself!
DUKE [Without]
Where is my Queen?

DUTCHESS
Quick let me fly to meet him,
Fly to my hero's breast.—
Velasquez seizes her and draws a dagger.

VELASQUEZ
Hold, madam, hold,
Thus I arrest your transports.

DUTCHESS
Barbarian! monster!

DUKE [Entering]
What sounds are these? Horror! Inhuman slave?
Turn thy fell pogniard here

VELASQUEZ
Approach not, stir not.
Or by the blackest furies hell ere loos'd,
This dagger drinks her blood.

DUKE
See, I obey,
I breathe not, stir not, I am rooted here.
Here will I grow for ages.

DUTCHESS
Oh my Juan!

DUKE
O horrible! Does Juan live for this?

Curs'd be the fatal fire that led my steps
To follow false ambition, while I left
To lurking robbers an unguarded prize;
This gem more worth than crowns or worlds can ransom

VELASQUEZ
Take back a name more foul, thou dark usurper
Was it for this, thy unsuspecting prince
With lavish bounty, to thy faithless hand
Trusted his royal functions? Thus to arm
'Gainst his own breast, thy black ingratitude.

DUKE
Must I endure it?

DUTCHESS
Out! false hypocrite!
Thy tyrants snares were found, his flimsy nets
To catch that precious life long since unravel'd,
Thy conscious cheek avows it.

VELASQUEZ
Be it so.—

DUTCHESS
Coward! Perfidious coward! Is it thus,
Thus you requite—

VELASQUEZ
Thy foolish pity—thus—
Hear me thou rebel—Is this woman dear?

DUKE
O heavens!

VELASQUEZ
Thy straining eyes, thy agonizing heart,
Thy life's inglorious dotage all proclaim it.

DUTCHESS
Peace, devil, peace, nor wound his generous soul
By taunts that fiends might blush at.

DUKE
Speak thy purpose.

VELASQUEZ
Then briefly thus—call off thy traiterous guards,

—The fruits of thy foul treason, every post,
Seiz'd by the midnight plots, thy rebel arms
Restore again to Spain—Back to the palace
Give me save conduct—To thy oaths I trust not;
It must be done this instant—leave my power
To intercede with Spain for thy full pardon,
And grace to all, whom thy ill-starr'd ambition
Led to this base revolt—Else, by my rage!
The boiling rage that works my soul to frenzy,
Thou shalt behold this beauteous bosom gor'd,
All over gash'd and mangled

DUTCHESS
Strike this instant!

DUKE
Hold, ruffian, hold!

DUTCHESS
Give me a thousand deaths;
Here let me fall a glorious sacrifice,
Rather than buy my life by such dishonour.
[To the **DUKE**]
If thy fond love accept these shameful terms,
That moment is my last—these hands shall end me.
[To **VELASQUEZ**]
Blood thirsty tyger, glut thy fury here.

VELASQUEZ
Her courage blasts my purpose [Aside] dost thou brave me

DUTCHESS
Defy thee—yes—feel, do I shrink or tremble?
Serene undaunted will I meet the blow;
But ev'ry drop that stains thy reeking hands,
In thy last pangs shall cry for vengeance on thee.
Furies shall seize thee, shake their scorpion whips,
And in thy deafen'd ears still hollow, murder.

VELASQUEZ
No more—Resolve—
[To the **DUKE**]
—Not Heaven itself can save her.
Ha! darkness cover me! he still alive!
Fate thou hast caught me—Every hope is lost.

[Enter **RAMIREZ** wounded, **ALMADA**, **RIBIRO**, **MENDOZA** and **OTHERS** following—The **DUKE** and **DUTCHESS** run to each others arms—**VELASQUEZ** is seized.

DUKE
I have thee once again, my heart's best treasure,
Sav'd from the vulture's talons—O dire fiend!

VELASQUEZ
Unhand me—No—though earth and hell conspire.

DUTCHESS
Blasphemer, down! and own a power above thee!

RIBIRO
Secure this monster—Read this paper, madam.
Returning from the charge we found that wretch
Stretch'd in our way and welt'ring in his blood;
Earnest he beg'd we shou'd commit to note
These few short words, and bear them to the Duke.
That done, he dragg'd his bleeding body on,
And came to die before him.

DUKE
Oh, Ramirez!
Ev'n in this day of joy my heart runs o'er
With sorrow for thy fate—What cruel hand?

RAMIREZ
—A villain's hand, yet Heaven directed it.
I have not strength to publish all my shame,
That roll contains it—This wide gaping wound,
My deep remorse, may expiate my crime;
But, Oh! that tempter—

DUKE
Ha! he faints, support him.
Thy crime, what crime?

RAMIREZ
Thy happier star prevail'd,
Else, hadst thou died even by the pious act
That seals our peace above.

DUKE
Merciful powers!

RAMIREZ
Yet ere I sink, speak comfort to my soul,
And bless me with forgiveness.

DUKE
Take it freely.

RAMIREZ
Enough, I die contented. He is led off

DUTCHESS
O my Juan,
Peruse that tale and wonder—Impious wretch,
Well might my heart stand still—my blood run cold,
And struggling nature murmur strong reluctance
Against my foolish pity—While I meant
To step between thee and the brandish'd bolt,
To rescue from the stroke of righteous justice
The foul suborner of my husband's murder.

VELASQUEZ
Curse on the coward's fears prevented it!
Wither these sinews that relax'd their hold,
And left thy feeble wing to soar above me,

DUKE
Hence with that villain—Drag him from my sight.—
Till aweful justice doom his forfeit life,
Let heaviest chains secure him—Hence, begone.

VELASQUEZ
Yes, in your gloomiest dungeons plunge me down.
Welcome congenial darkness—Horrors hail!
No more these loathing eyes shall view that sun,
Whose irksome beams light up thy pageant triumph.

[He is led off by **RIBIRO** and **OTHERS**.

DUKE
Thou ever present, all protecting power!
Thro' what dark clouds of thick involving danger
Thy watchful providence has led my steps?
The imagin'd woes that sunk me in despair,
Thou mad'st the wond'rous instruments to save me.

DUTCHESS
I feel, I own the high supremacy—
Yet have I much to ask—Thy victory—

DUKE
For that our thanks to this brave man are due.
He chose the post of danger, and expos'd

His dauntless breast against the stubborn force
Of steady northern courage.

ALMADA
Twice was I down,
And twice my prince's valour rescued me.

DUKE
For ever hallow'd be the well pois'd blade
That sav'd that reverend head.

DUTCHESS
Fortune was kind, Almada, to commit
Your safety to the arm you taught to conquer.

ALMADA
Henceforth I more shall prize that trifle life,
Since now I owe it to my sovereign's valour.

[Enter **RIBIRO.**

RIBIRO
Vengeance thy debt is paid—The tyrant's dead.

DUKE
Say'st thou? Velasquez!

RIBIRO
Aye, what was Velasquez
Dispers'd and mangled by the people's rage,
In bloody fragments stains a thousand hands;
Like ravenous wolves by eager famine pinch'd,
With worrying fangs they dragg'd him from my grasp,
And in my fight tore out his reeking entrails.

DUKE
His blood be on his head, and may his end,
Provok'd by crimes beyond the reach of pardon,
Strike terror to the souls of impious men,
Who own no God, but from his pow'r to punish.

EPILOGUE

By a FRIEND.
SPOKEN BY MRS. YATES.

Is it permitted in this age severe,
For female softness to demand a tear?
Is it allow'd in such censorious days,
For female virtue to solicit praise?
Dares manly sense, beneath a tender form,
Presume to dictate, and aspire to warm?
May so unnatural a being venture
As a true heroine on the stage to enter?
No, says a wit, made up of French grimaces,
Yet self-ordain'd the high-priest of the graces.
Women are play-things for our idle hours,
Their souls unfinish'd, and confin'd their pow'rs;
Loquacious, vain, by slight attentions won,
By flattery gain'd, and by untruths undone.
Or should some grave great plan engage their minds,
The first caprice can give it to the winds;
And the chief stateswoman of all the sex
Grows nervous, if a fop or pimple vex.
Injurious slanders!—in Louisa's air
Behold th' exemplar of a perfect fair;
Just, tho' aspiring; merciful, tho' brave;
Sincere, tho' politic; and tho' fond, no slave;
In danger calm, and smiling in success,
But as securing ampler means to bless.
Nor think, as Zeuxis, for a faultless piece,
Cull'd various charms from various nymphs of Greece,
Our bard has center'd in one beauteous whole,
The rays that gleam thro' many a separate soul.
On Britain's and Ierne's shores he saw
The models of the fair he dar'd to draw;
True virtue in these isles has fix'd her throne,
And many a bright Louisa is our own.